DIVIDED WE
STAND

HOW TO LOVE WHEN WE DISAGREE

Cover & Interior Design by Outskirts Studio

Produced by **Trueface**
Trueface.org
ISBN: 979-8-9860131-0-7

Printed in the United States.

CONTENTS

GETTING STARTED

Welcome to *Divided We Stand*. Disagreement can be uncomfortable and awkward for many of us. It can lead to hard conversations, to avoiding certain topics, and sometimes to ending a relationship all together. Many of these disagreements have led to division in the world and in the church. Jesus modeled what it looks like to love people with whom we disagree. As his followers, we are uniquely equipped to do the same. This study is designed to help you wade into the messiness of disagreement and unveil Christ's love and unity in a divided world.

You can find all the session videos and additional resources at *trueface.org/DWSstudy*. Simply sign up for a free account and choose the Divided We Stand course. Here you'll find the trailer for this course, which we recommend watching as a group to prepare for the study, the videos for each week's discussion, and short introductions to each of the participants.

Divided We Stand is structured similarly to other Trueface studies, which means that within each meeting you will go through three sections:

CONNECT

Spend time connecting with each other in order to deepen relationships.

LEARN

Use content to grow spiritually.

LIVE

Discuss and apply what you learned to your here-and-now lives so that you can live out and experience these truths.

HOW TO FACILITATE: We have provided recommended time frames to help you stay on track in your meetings. These time frames reference a sixty- or ninety-minute group meeting.

TRUEFACE

beyond the mask

Today's culture is perfecting the art and science of creating masks. Behind these masks, people are dying inside. We're here to change that.

Trueface equips people to experience the freedom of living beyond the mask, because behind the mask is the real you. When we increase trust in our relationships, we are able to experience being more authentically known and loved by God and others.

We hope to be a bridge for hundreds of thousands to experience the peace and freedom of the original good news by trusting God and others with their whole selves—the self behind the mask.

To learn more about Trueface, visit *trueface.org* or join the thousands of people living the Trueface life on social media.

Instagram: **@truefacelife**

Facebook: **@truefacecommunity**

Twitter: **@truefaced**

Trueface is a non-profit supported by people who have been impacted by the ministry. To help us create more resources like this one, visit *trueface.org/give.*

LOGISTICS

You'll find the videos and other additional resources for this study at *trueface.org/DWSstudy.* The videos and resources are free to use and are broken up by each meeting. Simply create a free account and sign up for the *Divided We Stand* course to get access to this content.

Below is a place for you to write down when you'll meet, where you'll meet, and the most important thing—who'll bring the food! Fill out this section with your group members in your first meeting.

MEETING 1:

Divided We Stand

Date: _____

Location: _____

Snacks: _____

MEETING 2:

This Is Who I Am

Date: _____

Location: _____

Snacks: _____

MEETING 3:

What About "Them"?

Date: _____

Location: _____

Snacks: _____

MEETING 4:

Love on Purpose

Date: _____

Location: _____

Snacks: _____

WEEK 1

DIVIDED WE STAND

MEETING TOGETHER

Have someone read this out loud:

Welcome to Divided We Stand. By choosing to do this study, you are already taking a brave step that many struggle with. Throughout these meetings, we will explore what love looks like when we disagree, and we will practice the skills of humility and curiosity along the way. In this first week, we'll spend some time getting in touch with why division matters, how we each respond to it, and where we want to go from here as we seek to live and love like Jesus did.

NOTES

CONNECT

THIS SECTION WILL TAKE ABOUT 20% OF YOUR TIME TOGETHER TODAY.

AS A GROUP:

- Pray:

  » Have someone pray to open this study. Invite the Holy Spirit to prepare your hearts to experience more of God's love, truth, and grace.

- Connect questions:

    » What is a way that you felt loved or supported in the last thirty days?

    » What hopes and/or concerns do you have for doing this study?

LEARN

 THIS SECTION WILL TAKE ABOUT 30% OF YOUR TIME TOGETHER TODAY.

> **WATCH THE "DIVIDED WE STAND" VIDEO.**
> You'll find this at *trueface.org/DWSstudy.*

LIVE

THIS SECTION WILL TAKE ABOUT 50% OF YOUR TIME TOGETHER TODAY.
In these Live sections, you will typically spend about half of your time on discussion and half of your time on application.

REFLECT:

First, have someone read the following passage of Jesus praying out loud:

John 17:13-36 NIV

"I am coming to you now, but I say these things while I am still in the world, so that they may have the full measure of my joy within them. I have given them your word and the world has hated them, for they are not of the world any more than I am of the world. My prayer is not that you take them out of the world but that you protect them from the evil one. They are not of the world, even as I am not of it. Sanctify them by the truth; your word is truth. As you sent me into the world, I have sent them into the world. For them I sanctify myself, that they too may be truly sanctified.

My prayer is not for them alone. I pray also for those who will believe in me through their message, that all of them may be one, Father, just as you are in me and I am in you. May they also be in us so that the world may believe that you have sent me. I have given them the glory that you gave me, that they may be one as we are one—I in them and you in me—so that they may be brought to complete unity. Then the world will know that you sent me and have loved them even as you have loved me.

Father, I want those you have given me to be with me where I am, and to see my glory, the glory you have given me because you loved me before the creation of the world.

Righteous Father, though the world does not know you, I know you, and they know that you have sent me. I have made you known to them, and will continue to make you known in order that the love you have for me may be in them and that I myself may be in them."

Then, spend one minute in silence individually as you pray this prayer:

God, thank you for pouring out your love and bringing me into complete unity with you. I want to glorify you in my life. Where are you inviting me to join you in loving others?

DISCUSS:

What does this mean to me?

Choose a few questions from the list below to process together. You don't need to discuss all of them, but choose the ones that stand out to you the most. It can be tempting to give the "right" or "expected" answer for these questions. Resist that urge! Try to be as honest and real as you can. Remember the ground rules as you move into discussion:

GROUND RULES:

1. Give each other grace.
2. Choose to value people more than issues.
3. Seek understanding, not agreement.

NOTES

QUESTIONS:

1 What stood out to you about the video discussion?

2 What are the main emotions that come up for you when you enter into difficult or divisive conversations?

3 The roundtable talked about avoiding disagreement because we . . .

   a. feel uncomfortable.

   b. don't want to find out we might be wrong.

   c. are concerned our proximity will be seen as agreeing with someone's choices.

Which of these resonate with you and why?

4 How was disagreement modeled in your family?

5 Where in your life might God be calling you to love even though it's uncomfortable?

6 Tommy shared that when we are only around people that are the same as us, we miss out on some of the depth of Christ. What do you think of this statement?

7 What is most difficult for you about this issue of division as a whole?

NOTES

APPLY:

What faith step is God inviting me to take?

Discussions can help us grow and learn, but we are also called to let Jesus transform our real, here-and-now lives. Spend some time as a group discussing how to take a first step this next week.

What is one practical, tangible way you can move toward love in the midst of division this week? Some ideas are below:

- Identify someone you usually disagree with, and commit to praying for them this week.

- Think of a person or a group of people on the "other side" of an issue. Try journaling or writing about them from God's perspective as someone he has watched and loved throughout their lives.

- Spend a little time researching an area you feel uncomfortable engaging with. Try to understand the "other side" of the issue.

- Think about one area of judgment or divisiveness in your life. Spend time in prayer asking God to help you see his eternal perspective on it.

- Does anything else come to mind? Be creative, but practical. Try to make it an actionable step in order to help integrate your actions with your beliefs.

How I'm going to live it out (writing it down will help you remember it):

How can the group come alongside you over the next week? Letting other people love, encourage, and walk with us is foundational in grace-filled relationships.

Look ahead to the Digging Deeper 1 material where we begin exploring how humility and trust in our identities unlock us to love. There are five sections for you to read between now and your next meeting. If you don't get to them, that's okay. You won't get as much time to process in this study, but don't let that keep you from engaging in your group.

PRAY TO CLOSE OUT THIS TIME TOGETHER.

NOTES

DIGGING DEEPER

Between now and your next meeting, read these five sections and reflect on the questions at the end. You can do them all at once, but we suggest breaking the five sections over multiple days to give yourself more processing time. This week we will explore how humility and trusting our identity help us love others the way Jesus did.

If you are not able to go through the five sections before your next meeting, **that's okay.** Don't let it stop you from connecting with your community.

PASSAGE FOR THE WEEK

2 Corinthians 5:14-21 NIV

For Christ's love compels us, because we are convinced that one died for all, and therefore all died. And he died for all, that those who live should no longer live for themselves but for him who died for them and was raised again.

So from now on we regard no one from a worldly point of view. Though we once regarded Christ in this way, we do so no longer. Therefore, if anyone is in Christ, the new creation has come: The old has gone, the new is here! All this is from God, who reconciled us to himself through Christ and gave us the ministry of reconciliation: that God was reconciling the world to himself in Christ, not counting people's sins against them. And he has committed to us the message of reconciliation. We are therefore Christ's ambassadors, as though God were making his appeal through us. We implore you on Christ's behalf: Be reconciled to God. God made him who had no sin to be sin for us, so that in him we might become the righteousness of God.

NOTES

SECTION 1

When we hear the word humility, we often think of thinking poorly of ourselves. We also might think of not thinking of ourselves at all—which makes it a difficult virtue, since thinking about the virtue automatically negates it!

Let's consider the opposite of humility, pride. Pride is trusting yourself more than anyone else. This shows up in our lives in all sorts of ways such as viewing ourselves higher than those around us, thinking we alone know best, or putting others down. In pride, we only trust ourselves with ourselves—no one else gets a say. But as scripture says in both James 4:6 and 1 Peter 5:5, "God resists the proud, but gives grace to the humble." God works through our trust in him. So when we are prideful, he must wait us out. We cannot receive the gift of grace when we don't think we need it.

Humility, on the other hand, is trusting God and others with ourselves. We begin our journey with Christ in humility, declaring that we need him. We trust him and believe that we cannot save ourselves. This is the wonder of salvation. We humbly accept a gift that we cannot earn or accomplish. We continue the rest of our Christian lives in humility, trusting God over ourselves as we learn to live and love like him.

But what about this "trusting others" part? Why can't we just trust God and ourselves and leave other people out of it? First, to be blunt, it simply doesn't work. The nature of blindspots is that we can't see them ourselves. We create our own echo chambers when we try to follow God completely alone. Second, God has made it abundantly clear in scripture that he delights in using other people to grow, challenge, and love us. Third, we can't receive people's love if we don't trust them. So, if we want to experience God and others' love, we must trust them. This is the heart of humility—trusting God and others with ourselves, instead of only trusting us with us. This kind of humility is the gateway to love.

REFLECTION QUESTIONS

In what areas do you feel like you trust God above yourself? In what areas do you feel like you trust yourself over God?

Who do you trust the most in your life? What makes them feel trustworthy?

Do you allow people to speak into your life? This might look like allowing them to give you trusted counsel on decisions, to speak challenging truth when you are blind to an issue, or to protect you in an area you are weak. Why or why not?

NOTES

SECTION 2

One area that is deeply intertwined with humility is our identity in Christ. When we trust God for our salvation, scripture tells us that we are made into new creations (2 Corinthians 5:17). We become identified as those who are fused with Christ forever. We are transformed into people who are called holy, righteous, beloved, and children of God. After this incredible moment of humility, we are no longer identified by our sin but by God's love. We are no longer sinners striving to become saints; we are saints who still sin. What preposterous, incredible, unbelievable, life-altering truth! A new identity and heart is ours based completely on what God has done instead of what we have done.

We may have felt this new identity in the first stages of our walk with Jesus, but then we stumbled a few times. We did things that we did before knowing Jesus. We found that we still had a lot of our old hangups and patterns, and we started to wonder if we were really changed. Maybe Jesus started the process, but now we've got to buck up and transform ourselves the rest of the way. We begin to trust our perspective and judgment over God's. We fear that we're not *really* a new creation because we can see the ways we need to grow. Slowly, we return to trusting ourselves with ourselves. Our identity is what we think it is—what we define it as—rather than what God says.

Here's the good news: our identity still lies securely in what God says about us even when our behaviors and fears shout that we're someone else! God says that we are saints, beloved, new, and holy regardless of our latest stumble. Do we trust God's view on our identity or our own? **In humility, we trust who God says we are, instead of who we say we are.** The more that we lean into trusting who God says we are, the more we begin to experience the freedom that he always meant for us to have.

REFLECTION QUESTIONS

What do you believe happened to you when you trusted Jesus for salvation? What happened to your heart?

What is the most challenging part of trusting who God says you are as a holy, new, beloved saint?

NOTES

SECTION 3

In our world, we have a lot of ways that we might define ourselves. Sometimes we define ourselves by our jobs. We might be a lawyer, plumber, teacher, homemaker, web designer, fast-food worker, or engineer. We can define ourselves in terms of our economic position. We see ourselves as wealthy, middle-class, in-poverty, or striving to move from one position to another. We view ourselves based on our relationships, whether we're married, single, divorced, a parent, grandchild, sibling, or friend. We define ourselves by our gender and sexual identity. We define ourselves by our culture, understanding our identity in the context of our family history, race, ethnicity, nationality, and education. We often define ourselves by our political leanings, whether it's left, right, center, or rejecting the spectrum all together. We identify based on our religious views even within the same faith, defining ourselves as fundamentalist, Episcopalian, progressive, or reformed. This list could go on and on.

These descriptors matter. They are all parts of you that help others connect with and understand you. They even help you understand you! These pieces are part of the incredible and necessary diversity in the body of Christ.

When you dig down past all of these descriptors, past your upbringing, talents, behaviors, relationships, and cultural context, what is your ultimate, deepest, truest identity? If you are in Christ, then you have your answer: Christ. At your core, your true, everlasting, primary identity is as one beloved by and secure in Jesus. When we get to sit with other Jesus followers who look, act, think, and experience life differently than us, we know that we share the same core identity. The beauty of these descriptor or secondary identities is that we get to see and experience the innumerable expressions of Christ in humanity. We do not stop being a middle-class accountant who is a parent—we are a righteous, fused-with-Christ saint who is expressed as a middle-class accountant who is a parent. As we value and press into the diversity of Jesus in each other, we get to experience more of his beauty and depth than we can possibly experience on our own.

REFLECTION QUESTIONS

What comes to mind when you think about how you identify yourself?

What are some secondary identities in others that you have preconceived notions about or struggle to connect with? Where did you learn that?

What is one of your secondary identities that you tend to elevate above your primary identity? Why do you think that is?

SECTION 4

What do humility and identity have to do with division? The answer: everything.

In humility, we live in the reality that God is God, and we are not. He seems to know a lot of things that we don't, and in fact he is the only one who sees things perfectly. In humility, we begin to take caution from the religious professionals of Jesus' day, who were quite sure that they alone saw things correctly and had it all figured out. Meanwhile, Jesus said that they completely missed the point. Humility reminds us that while we can have strong convictions, we are still only human, and our perspective could still be wrong.

In humility, it's not only God who knows things that we don't—other people know things as well! They can see blindspots and biases that we're totally unaware of and help us see from perspectives that we couldn't have on our own.

This humility gives birth to and sustains our new, primary identity. As we grow in trusting this identity, it allows us to open ourselves to both God and others in entirely new ways. We no longer have to fear finding out that we were wrong about something, because we know that we are secure and beloved. We can now be genuinely curious about our own biases and blindspots, trusting that they will show us areas where we can lean more into Christ. We are able to acknowledge these growth areas with less shame and more openness,

NOTES

29

excited for others to help us live out of our sainthood more fully as we trust who Christ has made us. We begin to see the ways God uses healthy division to multiply and diversify his body, like a growing tree with constant cell division leading to the growth and beauty of a forest.

As we humbly trust our true identity more and more, we discover that we can love across the aisle and lean into hard conversations. We are quick to say "I'm sorry," or, "Tell me more." We seek out different perspectives and experiences, genuinely considering their merit. We forgive with the overflowing grace of God, and we repent out of true sorrow. We are able to be more curious and less defensive than we thought possible because at the end of the day we know who we are and whose we are. This is freedom taking hold in the life of the saint. This is love being unlocked.

REFLECTION QUESTIONS

For you, how might resting in your primary identity affect how you approach people you disagree with?

Where do you find it easiest to live out of your true, God-given identity? Where do you find it hardest?

In what ways do you try to prove yourself in difficult conversations? By being right, avoiding the topic, trying to appease, or something else?

SECTION 5

We are not who we were even on our worst day.

We are no longer defined by our history, mistakes, hang ups, or addictions. We are no longer defined by our successes, accolades, social power, or attractiveness. We are defined by Christ. He has made us new creations.

Now that we are fused with Christ, we have him and his attributes bubbling up inside of us like an endless well of living water. The fruits of the Spirit come from trusting Christ, not through powering up or trying harder. That means that as we lean into him, we will find love, joy, peace, patience, kindness, goodness, faithfulness, gentleness, and self-control flourishing in us. It's our new nature—our new DNA in Christ. We will still have many times where we try to put on the old self with its comfortable habits, struggles, and destructive patterns. We will forget what's true and internally return to our old lives of slavery to sin. But the shackles are broken by the only one who could break them, and that remains true when we believe it and when we don't.

Today, let's try living like we believe it. Try living like we believe that these maddening behaviors and old hang ups are just old shadows of who we used to be working their way out of our systems like a bad cold. Try living like we believe that Christ has given us a new heart that is completely, utterly, and forever fused

NOTES

with him. We no longer have to strive for belonging and significance—it has all been accomplished on our behalf. Trust that "he who began a good work in you will carry it on to completion until the day of Christ Jesus." (Philippians 1:6)

REFLECTION

Take some time to really consider what this might mean for your life. How would today look different if you lived out of trusting your new identity instead of striving to create or maintain one? What lies does the enemy whisper when you lean into this truth? How might you invite Jesus into that?

NOTES

WEEK 2

THIS IS WHO I AM

MEETING TOGETHER

How do you see yourself? What is your posture as you enter disagreements? This week we will explore how humility and security in our identity in Christ have a huge impact on how we engage in potentially divisive conversations.

CONNECT

🕐 20% OF YOUR TIME

AS A GROUP:

- Pray to open this time together. Who wants to volunteer?

- Connect question:

  » What might a person close to you say is one of your strengths?

- Check-in questions:

  » What stood out to you this week, either from our conversation last time or the Digging Deeper material?

  » Last week we talked about practical, tangible ways that we could step into love in the midst of division. How did that play out this week?

LEARN

 30% OF YOUR TIME

> ▷ **WATCH THE "THIS IS WHO I AM" VIDEO.**
> You'll find this at *trueface.org/DWSstudy*.

LIVE

◑ **50% OF YOUR TIME (HALF OF THE TIME DISCUSSING, HALF OF THE TIME APPLYING.)**

REFLECT:

Have someone read the following passage out loud:

John 13:3-5 NIV

Jesus knew that the Father had put all things under his power, and that he had come from God and was returning to God; so he got up from the meal, took off his outer clothing, and wrapped a towel around his waist. After that, he poured water into a basin and began to wash his disciples' feet, drying them with the towel that was wrapped around him.

NOTES

Then, spend one minute in silence individually as you pray this prayer:

Jesus, you were perfectly humble even though you were God, and you were completely secure in your identity. Where are you inviting me to experience more humility? Where are you inviting me to trust you with my identity?

DISCUSS:

What does this mean to me?

Choose a **few questions** that jump out to you from the list below and process them as a group. Do your best to not give the answer you think you're supposed to—try to be as authentic and real as you can.

1. What stood out to you from the video discussion?

2. When you think of having a more humble posture in these tense issues, what emotions surface?

3. How difficult is it for you to admit that you contribute to the problem of division?

4 We all have blindspots and biases, and these require others to help us see what we're missing. Who has permission to do that in your life?

5 What are some biases or stereotypes that you might have? Where did you learn those?

6 What biases and blindspots might this group have? Whose perspective is missing?

7 How can we continue to remember our true identity in Christ when we become afraid?

APPLY:

What faith step is God inviting me to take?

Talking about humility and identity is one thing, but living it out in our daily lives is a whole other challenge! Thankfully, Jesus sustains and guides us into freedom, but that doesn't mean that the road isn't rocky sometimes. Move your group discussion toward how we can start living out of humility and our true identity by asking the following questions:

- How would your life look different if you trusted who God says you are instead of who you say you are?

- Where is God inviting you to be humbly curious about how you contribute to division? How might you lean into that discomfort this week?

NOTES

In this coming week's Digging Deeper material, we're going to explore how this humble curiosity overflows to other people, particularly to people who are different from us. What is one practical, tangible way that you can be humbly curious with yourself this week? Ideas to get you started:

- Invite someone you trust to help you explore your biases and blindspots (remember, we all have them). This should be someone who holds a different perspective than you in at least one area.

- Ask this humble question to someone important to you, "How am I affecting you?" Assure them that they won't pay the price for being honest (and make sure you hold that promise). Listen with the intent of understanding what blindspots you might have.

- Identify an area where you haven't listened to understand another's point of view, either because you wanted to make your point or because you avoided the conversation. Spend some time being curious about why you didn't listen to understand. What were you afraid of?

- If there has been a relationship or situation where you have contributed to division, either by avoiding hard conversations or using them to argue, contact someone you affected and sincerely apologize for your part—even if they hurt you, too. Humbly own your part of the conflict.

- Anything else come to mind? Be creative, but practical. Try to make it an actionable step in order to help integrate your actions with your beliefs.

How I'm going to live it out:

How can the group or one member in the group come alongside you in this?

Look ahead to the Digging Deeper 2 material where we begin exploring how curiosity and empathy move us toward each other in love. There are five sections for you to read through between now and your next meeting. If you don't get to them, that's okay. You won't get as much time to process, but don't let that keep you from engaging with your group.

PRAY TO CLOSE OUT THIS TIME TOGETHER.

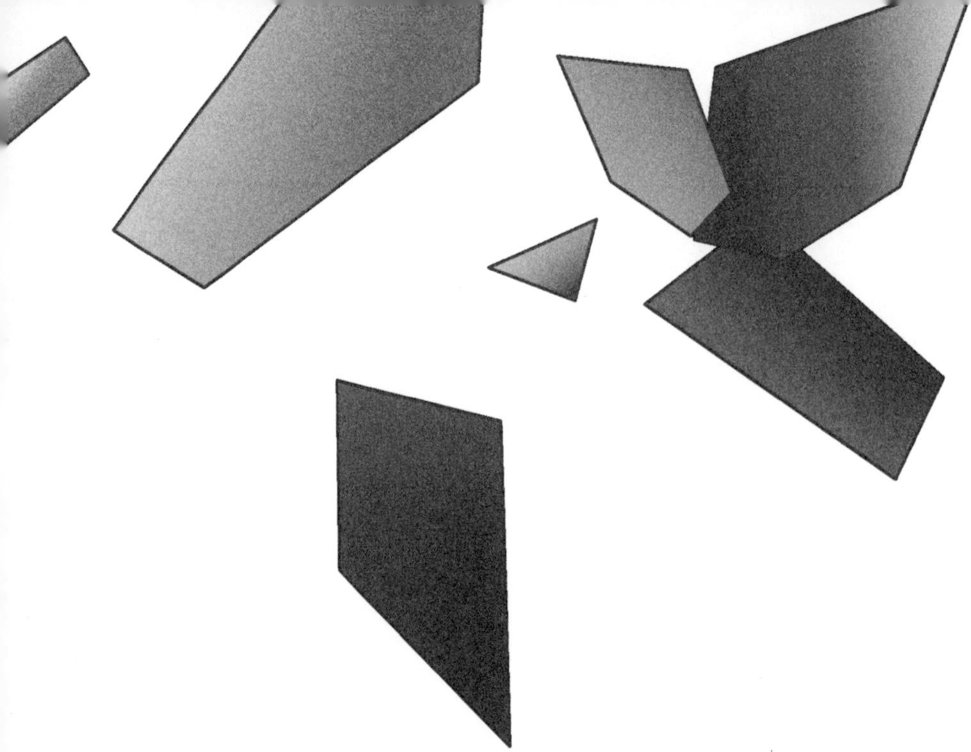

DIGGING DEEPER

Between now and your next meeting, read these five sections and reflect on the questions at the end. You can do them all at once, but we suggest breaking the five sections over multiple days to give yourself more processing time. This week we will explore how curiosity and empathy move us toward each other in love.

If you are not able to go through the five sections before your next meeting, **that's okay.** Don't let it stop you from connecting with your community.

PASSAGE FOR THE WEEK

John 4:5-30 NIV

So he came to a town in Samaria called Sychar, near the plot of ground Jacob had given to his son Joseph. Jacob's well was there, and Jesus, tired as he was from the journey, sat down by the well. It was about noon.

When a Samaritan woman came to draw water, Jesus said to her, "Will you give me a drink?" (His disciples had gone into the town to buy food.)

The Samaritan woman said to him, "You are a Jew and I am a Samaritan woman. How can you ask me for a drink?" (For Jews do not associate with Samaritans.)

Jesus answered her, "If you knew the gift of God and who it is that asks you for a drink, you would have asked him and he would have given you living water."

"Sir," the woman said, "you have nothing to draw with and the well is deep. Where can you get this living water? Are you greater than our father Jacob, who gave us the well and drank from it himself, as did also his sons and his livestock?"

Jesus answered, "Everyone who drinks this water will be thirsty again, but whoever drinks the water I give them will never thirst. Indeed, the water I give them will become in them a spring of water welling up to eternal life."

The woman said to him, "Sir, give me this water so that I won't get thirsty and have to keep coming here to draw water."

He told her, "Go, call your husband and come back."

"I have no husband," she replied.

Jesus said to her, "You are right when you say you have no husband. The fact is, you have had five husbands, and the man you now have is not your husband. What you have just said is quite true."

"Sir," the woman said, "I can see that you are a prophet. Our ancestors worshiped on this mountain, but you Jews claim that the place where we must worship is in Jerusalem."

"Woman," Jesus replied, "believe me, a time is coming when you will worship the Father neither on this mountain nor in Jerusalem. You Samaritans worship what you do not know; we worship what we do know, for salvation is from the Jews. Yet a time is coming and has now come when the true worshipers will worship the Father in the Spirit and in truth, for they are the kind of worshipers the Father seeks. God is spirit, and his worshipers must worship in the Spirit and in truth."

The woman said, "I know that Messiah" (called Christ) "is coming. When he comes, he will explain everything to us."

Then Jesus declared, "I, the one speaking to you—I am he."

Just then his disciples returned and were surprised to find him talking with a woman. But no one asked, "What do you want?" or "Why are you talking with her?"

Then, leaving her water jar, the woman went back to the town and said to the people, "Come, see a man who told me everything I ever did. Could this be the Messiah?" They came out of the town and made their way toward him.

NOTES

SECTION 1

Each of us have had our own unique experiences on this planet. We were born in specific places and times, to particular people, and into one-of-a-kind contexts. Our lives have been shaped by relationships, pain, joy, geography, ethnicity, culture, and more. There are no two humans that have lived the same story, and that is an incredible, beautiful truth.

These unique stories, however, also create biases and blind spots. Every human has them. According to what we have learned and experienced, our own personal makeup, and our cultural context, we have a particular perspective on the world. This means that we don't have everyone else's perspective! We certainly don't have God's full perspective, and that simply means we're missing some things.

Why does this feel so frightening to admit? Many of us may feel that acknowledging we have biases must mean that we are terrible people because only terrible people have biases, right? No. We have prejudices and biases by the very nature of us being limited humans! We are called to continuously be curious about what they might be and how we can expand our perspective. But we should never be ashamed to admit that we, *like all people*, have them.

This is another area where our identity is deeply important. If we are growing more and more convinced that Christ has indeed created us as new, holy, righteous saints, then we do not need to be afraid of admitting places where we need some work. It's okay to curiously ask, "What might my biases be? Where might I have some blind spots?" It no longer has a bearing on our worth or our acceptableness. Instead, it becomes an opportunity to grow in loving others well.

REFLECTION QUESTIONS

How does it feel to admit, even to yourself, that you have biases and blind spots simply by being human? What do you think might be driving that feeling?

NOTES

How have you seen other people model being curious about blind spots and biases, either positive or negative?

Based on your own knowledge of yourself, what might be some of your biases? These might look like assumptions about other people or groups of people.

SECTION 2

A tricky part of our blind spots and biases is that we cannot work on them alone. We don't know what we don't know. And while being curious about the biases we can spot on our own can be very helpful, we still need other people's help. We return to humility—trusting God and others with ourselves.

We have these blind spots and biases because our story has given us unique perspectives, and that means we need people with different stories to help us see from their point of view. While we can learn from anyone who is willing, seeking out people that are similar to you can often simply confirm your own biases—this is the definition of an echo chamber. Someone who grew up in a very different neighborhood, family, religion, socioeconomic status, or culture will see the world differently from you (and have their own biases too). Becoming curious and brave enough to ask for their help in exploring your blind spots can yield tremendous fruit.

Of course, this first takes a relationship of trust. We are not encouraging you to reach out to someone you don't know to ask for help. Trust is paramount for this kind of vulnerable conversation, and trust takes time and effort to build. If you don't feel that you have anyone you trust who sees the world differently from you, watch for Sections 4 and 5 this week. As you lean into these hard conversations, remember that you are a righteous, beloved child of the King, even as you open yourself up to another. He's got you!

NOTES

REFLECTION QUESTIONS

Who do you trust enough to ask them to help you see your biases and blind spots, maybe even just around a particular issue?

Do you typically surround yourself with people that see the world the same way as you? How might this be affecting your awareness of your biases and blind spots?

How could you reach out to someone who has a different story than you and begin learning from them?

NOTES

SECTION 3

Think about one group of people that you disagree with around a particular issue. What are your assumptions of those people? Are they misled by someone? Are they simply foolish, or put more bluntly, stupid? Or perhaps they are evil, actively seeking to harm or damage? These are the narratives often pushed in the public arena. And most likely, the people on the other side of this issue have some of the same assumptions about you!

However, people often have very good reasons for their views. They have had experiences that convince them they're true. Most often, from their perspective this is the rational, moral view on the issue. We might deeply disagree with them, but in humility in Christ we can find ourselves leaning in and asking a beautiful question, "What causes them to see it differently?"

That question can be incredibly disarming, especially if we are courageous enough to ask them directly. When we start to be curious about what we don't know and what we might be missing, it naturally leads us into conversations where our goal is to *understand*, not argue. These curious conversations sound like, "Tell me more," "I never saw it that way," "I'd like to think about that more," and, "I can really see why that's your perspective." **We know that we have really listened to understand when we are able to explain their position back to them in a way that they would fully support.** This is not saying that you agree with them.

NOTES

53

This is saying that you have taken the time to respect their views and truly understand them. Now if you choose to share your view on the issue, you will likely have a far different reception than if you barreled in without understanding their side. Genuine curiosity is remarkably disarming.

REFLECTION QUESTIONS

When you think about an issue that you feel strongly about and imagine trying to truly understand the other side, what emotions come up for you?

Try writing out how the other side sees this issue in a way that they would fully endorse.

Reflect on the above exercise. Was that difficult? Do you need more information? Does someone come to mind that might help you better understand a different perspective?

NOTES

SECTION 4

Consider your life journey up to today. First,
set the scene, such as time and place in history,
neighborhood, nation, and family culture. What are
some of the pivotal moments between birth and today
that have shaped you? Who has been most influential
in your life, both growing up and now?

All of these—and far more—shape how we see the
world. If others in our lives knew our whole story,
it would greatly help them understand who we are
today. The same goes for other people. Last section
we talked about listening to really understand
someone else's view on a particular divisive issue.
Today we step deeper, becoming curious about the
person themselves because **the enemy of prejudice is
proximity.**

The person on the other side of an issue also
has a family history filled with its unique joys
and brokenness. They likely went to school and
experienced classmates who were similar or different,
kind or cruel. They had people who deeply influenced
them and experiences that deeply shaped their
understanding of themselves and the world. They
have laughed, cried, and tried to make it through the
world. And if we could really step into their shoes
and understand the life they have lived—their unique
perspective on the world that has been forged out
of a thousand moments—we might find ourselves
sitting back and saying, "You know, if I had lived your

life, I might see it the same way you do." And even more profoundly, we might find our empathy and compassion overflowing for this person in all of their triumphs and terrible pains.

REFLECTION QUESTIONS

Why do we avoid getting to know people on the other side of an issue in a deep and personal way?

NOTES

Who, specifically, can you reach out to with the goal of hearing their unique story and better understanding them? What might be some barriers to reaching out?

SECTION 5

When we genuinely want to know and be known by people who are different from us, we begin to build relationships of trust. Brick by brick we create a relational space where we are able to learn and grow together—a space that is defined by grace and embedded with curiosity. When we talk about getting to know someone different than you, we aren't talking about a one-and-done conversation. We're talking about forging an ongoing relationship.

This means that the first conversation might not go well. You may reach out to someone who is unwilling to talk with you, or they may not be open to answering a particular question. If you are pursuing a relationship with someone who has been marginalized, they may be weary of answering questions, or they may be guarded about sharing their story. That's okay. Let grace abound in that response as well. Assure them that you want to know them as a person, and that you'd like to be known by them, too. This isn't a one-way-street. In order for this to be a true relationship, you need to let them know, support, and understand you, too.

Jesus gives us amazing examples of what it looks like to have relationships with people with whom we disagree. He lived life among tax collectors, prostitutes, religious elitists, and societal rejects. He ate with them, talked with them, and loved them exactly where they were. He also let them know and love him in return! So follow your savior into the kind of love that is in for the long haul, suffers with others, and knows that we need to both give and receive love. The enemy of prejudice is proximity—move in!

REFLECTION QUESTIONS

Which is more challenging for you, to get to know those that are different from you or to be known by them?

Take a moment to imagine living a life like Jesus, surrounded by people of all kinds of backgrounds and walks of life. What emotions come up for you?

NOTES

WEEK 3

WHAT ABOUT "THEM"?

MEETING TOGETHER

We're growing to be more humbly curious about ourselves, but what about "them"—those other people on the "wrong" side of an issue? We see ourselves as reasonable and thoughtful, but we see them as the ones stirring up conflict, having views that make no sense, or maybe being just plain evil. We've agreed that we're part of the issue of division . . . but what about "them"?

CONNECT

20% OF YOUR TIME

- Pray to open this time together. Who wants to volunteer?

- Connect question:

  » When was the last time someone seemed genuinely curious about you, your views, or your experiences? How did that feel?

- Check-in questions:

  » Last week we talked about practical, tangible ways that we could be humbly curious with ourselves. How did that play out this past week? If you didn't take the step you chose last week, what do you think held you back?

» What stood out to you this week, either from our conversation last time or the Digging Deeper material?

LEARN

 20% OF YOUR TIME

>  **WATCH THE "WHAT ABOUT THEM" VIDEO.**
> You'll find this at *trueface.org/DWSstudy.*

REFLECT:

Have someone read the following passage out loud:

John 13:34-35 NIV

"A new command I give you: Love one another. As I have loved you, so you must love one another. By this everyone will know that you are my disciples, if you love one another."

Then, spend one minute in silence individually as you pray this prayer:

Lord, teach me what it means to be known by the way I love others. Where are you inviting me to love more like you?

NOTES

LIVE

🌓 **60% OF YOUR TIME**

This week we will have you discuss the video and then move into a group activity to practice putting these ideas into action.

DISCUSS:

Choose a few questions that jump out to you from the list below and process them as a group.

1 What stood out to you from the video discussion?

2 When have you experienced someone assuming either what you think or why you think it? How did that feel?

3 How do humility and identity set the foundation for curious conversations?

4 Why might we want people to think, act, or believe the same as us?

5 What emotions come up when you think about asking someone on the other side of an issue to help you understand their perspective?

6 What conversations have you been avoiding and why?

PRACTICE:

Being humbly curious with ourselves can be challenging enough, but stepping out and being curious about other people can feel downright terrifying. This is a place where rooting ourselves firmly in our identity in Christ is deeply necessary, for out of that flows the courage and peace we need to be bridge-builders and reconcilers. Jesus calls us to a life of love lived out. This includes us risking hard conversations for the sake of others. Put another way, he calls us to have some skin in the game.

Practice having some curious conversations right here in your group. Here are two ways you could do this:

1 Pair off with individuals who aren't as familiar with each other. Set a timer for fifteen minutes, and practice asking curious questions about a more sensitive topic to try to better understand each other. Remember what Tyler said about honoring and holding space for stories—this is an investment in a relationship, not a checklist!

2 Have two people volunteer who have different opinions about something (remember, opinions are held more loosely than convictions or beliefs, so they're a good place to start). Then, practice having a curious conversation, trying to understand the other person's view on that subject. The group can help if they get stuck. Then, choose two others to practice.

NOTES

If neither of these fits your group, what is another way you can practice these brave, curious conversations right now? How can you practice pursuing understanding?

APPLY:

This week we encourage you to let this overflow into your life outside the group. Choose one person that you can practice a curious conversation with in the next week.

Who I am going to seek greater understanding with:

How can the group encourage each other to take this courageous step?

PRAY TO CLOSE OUT THIS TIME TOGETHER.

NOTES

DIGGING DEEPER

Between now and your next meeting, read these five sections and reflect on the questions at the end. You can do them all at once, but we suggest breaking the five sections over multiple days to give yourself more processing time. This week we will explore how dignity and justice are the natural outpour of loving others the way Christ does—even those with whom we disagree.

If you are not able to go through the five sections before your next meeting, **that's okay.** Don't let it stop you from connecting with your community.

PASSAGE FOR THE WEEK

Luke 10:25-37 NIV

On one occasion an expert in the law stood up to test Jesus. "Teacher," he asked, "what must I do to inherit eternal life?"

"What is written in the Law?" he replied. "How do you read it?"

He answered, "'Love the Lord your God with all your heart and with all your soul and with all your strength and with all your mind'; and, 'Love your neighbor as yourself.'"

"You have answered correctly," Jesus replied. "Do this and you will live."

But he wanted to justify himself, so he asked Jesus, "And who is my neighbor?"

In reply Jesus said: "A man was going down from Jerusalem to Jericho, when he was attacked by robbers. They stripped him of his clothes, beat him and went away, leaving him half dead. A priest happened to be going down the same road, and when he saw the man, he passed by on the other side. So too, a Levite, when he came to the place and saw him, passed by on the other side. But a Samaritan, as he traveled, came where the man was; and when he saw him, he took pity on him. He went to him and bandaged his wounds, pouring on oil and wine. Then he put the man on his own donkey, brought him to an inn and took care of him. The next day he took out two denarii and gave them to the innkeeper. 'Look after him,' he said, 'and when I return, I will reimburse you for any extra expense you may have.'

"Which of these three do you think was a neighbor to the man who fell into the hands of robbers?"

The expert in the law replied, "The one who had mercy on him."

Jesus told him, "Go and do likewise."

NOTES

SECTION 1

Have you ever come into a movie theater late and missed the first part of a film—maybe the first ten or fifteen minutes? It's difficult to know what's happening, isn't it?

In the same way, it's difficult for us to understand how much we matter to God unless we go back to the beginning when he set all of this in motion. In Genesis (the beginning), God created the earth, sky, trees, and animals. And then God created human beings. We are unlike anything else he made. This is how the writer of Genesis summarizes:

"So God created mankind in his own image, in the image of God he created them; male and female he created them."

Genesis 1:27 NIV

This concept is referred to as imago dei, which is translated in English as "Image of God." The Creator placed himself in what he created. All people have the DNA of God inside of them. This means that even though human beings are fallen and broken, **they are still image-bearers.** That includes the people you disagree with, you don't like, and who look, act, and believe differently than you! They are deeply valued by God, just like you.

REFLECTION QUESTIONS

How does understanding imago dei change the way we see people that we disagree with?

Have you ever looked for a reflection of God in the people you disagree with? Why or why not?

What's one way that you can assign value to other people even when you disagree with them?

NOTES

SECTION 2

God doesn't love us because he has to. He loves us because he wants to. He delights in us! We are his handiwork—made uniquely—and he enjoys his creation. He has chosen to love us, and nothing can separate us from his love.

God didn't wait to love us until we got our act together, figured things out, or had perfect theology. No, as Romans 5:8 says,

"But God demonstrates his own love for us in this: While we were still sinners, Christ died for us."

Think about that for a moment. Christ felt that we were worth his very life even in our darkest moments. This wasn't based on our behavior or our beliefs. He showed that he valued us just as we are more than his life.

This means that those who look, act, think, and believe differently are worth his life as well. Richard Mouw says this powerfully in his book *Uncommon Decency*.

"All human beings are God's handiwork. Each person is a very precious work of divine art. To make light of an artist's work within the artist's earshot is a cruel thing to do. To demean one of God's most precious artworks when God is listening—and he always is—crudely dishonors the divine artist."

Do we treat others, including those we most disagree with, as though they were worth Christ's life? As we deepen our understanding of this truth that all people are made in the image of God and that Christ died for all, it begins to transform the way we value, honor, and defend all humans. Even those with whom we disagree!

REFLECTION QUESTIONS

Who do you struggle to value the way Christ does?

If you chose to treat and value other people as though they are worth Christ's life, what's one thing you would do differently?

SECTION 3

Let's all admit something obvious. We're happy when other people do what we want. We like it when people see things our way.

The problem, however, is that people don't always do what we want. They don't act like we would if we were in their shoes. They don't see eye to eye with us. And sometimes, we spend a lot of time and energy trying to get them on the same page as us. We use tactics like coercing, arguing, persuading, manipulating, nagging, berating, and rallying people to our side just to name a few.

It's easy to forget that it is the work of God through his Holy Spirit that changes, convinces, and convicts. We can love and provide our understanding, but it isn't our job to argue someone into the Kingdom (or into our view on an issue).

So, what is our job? Take a look at this verse in the Message translation of the Bible:

"Live a lover's life, circumspect and exemplary, a life Jesus will be proud of: bountiful in fruits from the soul, making Jesus Christ attractive to all, getting everyone involved in the glory and praise of God."
Philippians 1:11 MSG

God loves us when we don't earn it. He died for us when we didn't deserve it. He extends grace to us that we can't fathom. He works on us and in us, even through our brokenness. So, let's let God be God! We get to focus on making him attractive to all, on loving with the bountiful fruits of the Spirit, and on giving him glory in all circumstances.

REFLECTION QUESTIONS

Whose responsibility is it to change minds and hearts? Why is this difficult to accept?

Does your salvation rest on understanding God and all of his ways perfectly? Why or why not?

NOTES

Do you need to make sure that people think "correctly" (which means like you) for God to work in them? Explain your answer.

What would it look like for you to make Jesus attractive to others?

NOTES

SECTION 4

Like we already said, humans are different from all of God's other creations. *Imago Dei* is what sets us apart. Because every person is created in the image of God, they have the right to be viewed with value and treated with respect and dignity.

The problem, as we all know, is that all throughout history humanity has failed to do this. Civilizations have preyed on vulnerable people for their own benefit. People have been categorized as less-than-human and victimized for personal gain. In one way or another, we're all guilty of this.

Into all of that stepped—and still steps—Jesus. When he was on Earth, he loved the poor, oppressed, outcasts, and sinners. He sought out vulnerable people, loved them, protected them, and spoke worth and value into their lives. He revealed the heart of God, which was to restore justice to ones who couldn't restore it for themselves. This is called restorative justice, and we are invited to join him in this incredible kingdom work.

This is what the book of Proverbs says:

"Speak up for those who cannot speak for themselves,
*   for the rights of all who are destitute.*
Speak up and judge fairly;
*   defend the rights of the poor and needy."*
Proverbs 31:8-9 NIV

Justice is a big deal to God. He cares about the vulnerable, destitute, poor, and needy. He talks about this throughout scripture, again and again returning to this theme. We have a broken lens of how to treat each other. Not only is God seeking to heal our view of others, he's also asking us to participate with him in their restoration.

REFLECTION QUESTIONS

How would you define restorative justice?

NOTES

If Jesus were on Earth today, who do you think he would move toward?

In what ways would Jesus be most controversial to the church today?

SECTION 5

"Is not this the kind of fasting I have chosen:
to loose the chains of injustice
*   and untie the cords of the yoke,*
to set the oppressed free
*   and break every yoke?*
Is it not to share your food with the hungry
*   and to provide the poor wanderer with shelter—*
when you see the naked, to clothe them,
*   and not to turn away from your own flesh and blood?*
Then your light will break forth like the dawn,
*   and your healing will quickly appear;*
then your righteousness will go before you,
*   and the glory of the Lord will be your rear guard.*
Then you will call, and the Lord will answer;
*   you will cry for help, and he will say: Here am I."*

Isaiah 58:6-9 NIV

God works our restoration in the midst of restoring others. He heals our hearts as we pour them out for those around us. We experience more of our true identity as we join him in his sacrificial love.

We innately crave a bigger story to play a role in. We need a bigger existence than just our families and ourselves. Out of his love and grace, God has called us to join him in restoring justice to the oppressed around us. What would it look like for you and I to make a concerted effort to lift up the vulnerable in our communities? The new heart that God has given us is made for loving others—let's ask him to enflame our new hearts for those around us. Let's invite him to break our hearts with what breaks his heart. Let's boldly call on him to bring people into our lives who need help so that "our light will break forth like the dawn."

To get your mind moving in that direction, here are some starting ideas. Ask God to direct your path in the direction that he wants it to go, and to bring to mind other ideas for your context:

- Become a foster care parent or babysitter.

- Become a mentor in a local school.

- Donate money to organizations that fight sex trafficking.

- Befriend someone who's in a marginalized or vulnerable state right now.

- Partner with school social workers to identify children who come to school hungry. Participate in bringing them food.

- Donate blood.

- Consistently visit a nursing home.

NOTES

REFLECTION QUESTIONS

What's one way that you can be involved in restorative justice?

What will hold you back from doing that?

How do you think participating in restorative justice will propel your faith?

WEEK 4

LOVE ON PURPOSE

MEETING TOGETHER

When Jesus came to live among us and to die for our sins, he made our problems his problems. And we've created a lot of problems! God continually invites us in scripture to join his work of restorative justice, of lifting up the vulnerable and the marginalized to their rightful place of valued images of God. But what does that really look like in practice?

CONNECT

🕐 **30% OF YOUR TIME**

- Pray to begin this time together. Who wants to volunteer?

- Warm-up question:

  » What is something that has stood out to you personally over the past four weeks?

- Check-in questions:

  » What came up for you over the past week, either from our meeting together or from your Digging Deeper reading?

  » Last week we chose individuals we wanted to have a curious conversation with. How did that go?

LEARN

 20% OF YOUR TIME

 WATCH THE "LOVE ON PURPOSE" VIDEO.
You'll find this at *trueface.org/DWSstudy.*

REFLECT:

*Read the following passage from Isaiah 58:6-12
NIV out loud:*

*"Is not this the kind of fasting I have chosen:
to loose the chains of injustice
    and untie the cords of the yoke,
to set the oppressed free
    and break every yoke?
Is it not to share your food with the hungry
    and to provide the poor wanderer with shelter—
when you see the naked, to clothe them,
    and not to turn away from your own flesh and blood?
Then your light will break forth like the dawn,
    and your healing will quickly appear;
then your righteousness will go before you,
    and the glory of the Lord will be your rear guard.
Then you will call, and the Lord will answer;
    you will cry for help, and he will say: Here am I.
If you do away with the yoke of oppression,
    with the pointing finger and malicious talk,
and if you spend yourselves in behalf of the hungry
    and satisfy the needs of the oppressed,
then your light will rise in the darkness,
    and your night will become like the noonday.*

NOTES

The Lord will guide you always;
  he will satisfy your needs in a sun-scorched land
  and will strengthen your frame.
You will be like a well-watered garden,
  like a spring whose waters never fail.
Your people will rebuild the ancient ruins
  and will raise up the age-old foundations;
you will be called Repairer of Broken Walls,
  Restorer of Streets with Dwellings."

Spend five minutes in silence individually reflecting on this passage.

NOTES

LIVE

◑ 50% OF YOUR TIME

DISCUSS:

What does this mean to me?

Choose a few questions that jump out to you from the list below to process as a group.

1. What stood out to you in the video discussion?

2. How does it change your posture when you remember that the person you most disagree with was made in the image of God?

3. Jennifer and Juni shared stories of people speaking words of value to someone vulnerable. Has someone ever done this for you? Who might you do this for?

4. Where in your life do you pass by someone in need of justice like the priest and Levite in the parable of the Good Samaritan?

5. Tommy shared that compassion isn't just service to but suffering with others. What fears come up for you with that?

6. What is a barrier or fear that prevents you from participating in justice?

7. What would it look like to stretch yourself to serve and care for someone in a sacrificial way that costs you?

APPLY:

What faith step is God inviting me to take?

Long ago, humans broke things in this world, deciding some people were more valuable than others. God has been working to set it right ever since, and he is inviting us to join him in this incredible work. This usually starts in our micro worlds with loving the people around us sacrificially and seeking to use whatever resources we have been blessed with to bless others. **How can you participate in God's restorative justice this week?** Talk about it practically and tangibly. Here are some ideas to get you started:

- Join an organization that provides mentorship to low-income teens.

- Offer to deliver groceries or provide yard maintenance to elderly neighbors.

- Volunteer with local organizations that help refugees or immigrants get settled in your area.

- Offer to babysit for single-parent households.

- Get involved in a community garden.

- Participate in community work days or organize one yourself!

- Anything else come to mind? Every situation is different and may require different steps.

How I'm going to live it out:

What could this group do together to lift up others
and participate in restorative justice?

PRAY TO CLOSE OUT THIS TIME TOGETHER.

DIGGING DEEPER

"Finally, brothers and sisters, rejoice! Strive for full restoration, encourage one another, be of one mind, live in peace. And the God of love and peace will be with you."

2 Corinthians 13:11 NIV

We serve a God who delights in the diversity of his image in humankind. He designed us to be unique and different from each other and to be united in our love for him and for one another. We get the incredible privilege of displaying the love of Christ in the midst of division, and in joining him as he ushers in a kingdom of justice, love, and unity. Go and live!

If you're looking for more resources head to *Trueface.org.*

We have additional books, studies, and experiences to help you continue building high-trust communities of grace and inviting others to experience this life alongside you. You can also connect with thousands of others living the Trueface life on social media:

Instagram: @truefacelife

Facebook: @truefacecommunity

Twitter: @truefaced

CONTRIBUTORS

The executive editor and writer of this study was Brittany Sawrey, Trueface's Director of Content and Executive Editor of *Two Roads*, *Crazy Making*, and *Healing Relationships*.

ROBBY ANGLE, LPC

Robby Angle serves as the President and CEO of Trueface. He lives in Dawsonville, Georgia with his wife, Emily, and their eight children. Prior to Trueface, Robby served for over seven years at North Point Community Church in Atlanta, Georgia as the Director of Adult Ministry Environments and Director of Men's Groups. Robby led group counseling as a Licensed Clinical Mental Health Counselor and served with Samaritan's Purse in Pakistan and Myanmar overseeing international disaster response teams. Angle holds a certificate in biblical studies and degrees in business and counseling.

TYLER BURNS

Pastor Tyler Burns is a pastor, podcaster, TV show host, writer, and cultural commentator. He currently serves as the Lead Pastor of All Nations Worship Assembly in Pensacola, Florida. He has previously served in Youth Ministry and Discipleship Ministry for ten years. He is also the President of The Witness: A Black Christian Collective, an organization that seeks to encourage, educate, and empower Black Christians. Tyler hosts The Witness flagship podcast *Pass the Mic*, a podcast garnering over six million downloads. Witness has created safe space and inspiration for thousands of Black Christians around the world. He also serves as Vice President of Brand and Story at Chasing Justice.

Tyler is known for putting words to the lived experiences of his people. As an accomplished writer, he has written for publications such as The Washington Post, The Witness, and been featured in The Atlantic, Christianity Today, The Christian Post, and Religion News. Tyler has spoken for many global platforms, including The Justice Conference, The Justice Conference in South Africa, Q Ideas, Howard University Divinity School, among others. In his personal life, he is married to the love of his life, Mylena, and has two children, Trinity and Benaiah.

JUNI FELIX

Juni Felix is a member of New York Times Bestselling author Dr. BJ Fogg's Stanford Behavior Design Teaching Team, bestselling author of *You are Worth the Work: Moving Forward from Trauma to Faith*, a C.S. Lewis Institute Fellow, speaker, podcaster, and Midday Host for Moody Radio in Chicago. As a Tiny Habits Coach who has long used the method to help others transform lives and relationships with God, Juni has gone on to be a leader in the church. Through her speaking, broadcasting, and podcasting ministries, she is an encourager to people around the world.

Highly awarded for volunteer and community service, she's a technologist specializing in Behavior Design, assisting innovators from varied industries in the creation of collaborative teams, community minded products, systems, and services to make the world a better place. As a presenting author at the Thirteenth Annual Persuasive Technology Conference, she shared ideas for the Caring, Feeling, and Understanding Cities of the Future. She loves to travel the world collecting stories of hope. She also loves hiking and playing hours of video games. Her family motto is 'Always Pray - Always Play - and Never Give Up!' You can follow her ongoing global adventures at *JuniFelix.com*.

JENNIFER JUKANOVICH

Jennifer is a current doctoral candidate in the Global Leadership and Change program at Pepperdine University. She also coaches nonprofit boards through the M.J. Murdock Charitable Trust. Most recently, Jennifer served as Vice President for Student Life at Gordon College. Before joining the Gordon College administration in 2013, she lived and worked in Rwanda, where she served as communications director for a USAID project, co-founded a Rwandan-women-owned business, volunteered extensively with orphans and their caregivers, and launched a preschool and bi-yearly youth camps.

From 1998 to 2006, she served as the Founder and Executive Director of The Vine, a national gathering that brought thousands of young adults together across different Christian traditions. From 1994 to 1997, she served as a program associate for President Clinton's religious liaison and the Renaissance Weekends. She is a 1994 graduate of Gordon College and earned a Master's in Theology from Fuller Theological Seminary in 2003. Jennifer is active on the Boston Higher Education Resource Center and Teachers Training Together boards. She co-hosts the Forum on the Future of Education in Africa Post-COVID-19 through the International Community for Collaborative Content Creation. She is also an active community member at Trinity Northshore, an Anglican Church on Boston's Northshore. Jennifer and her husband, Dano, live in Wenham, Massachusetts with their three children.

TOMMY NIXON

Tommy Nixon has been leading as UYWI's Chief Executive Officer since 2018. Prior to UYWI, Tommy was a Founder and Executive Director of Solidarity, a nonprofit organization that strengthens urban communities, as well as the founding pastor at One Life City Church. He is passionate about helping urban leaders lead from a place of depth with God while having a dynamic impact in the kingdom on the local and global scale.

Tommy is also the host of *The Future is Here* podcast which is a deep dive into the future of the Church in a world that is increasingly young, urban, and multi-ethnic. He is also the creator and host of *The Radical Middle* show that helps believers embrace tension to bring change to this world.

𝍈 TRUEFACE

SMALL GROUP STUDIES

EMBARK

Our resource for starting a transformational small group, *Embark* is the companion group guide to *The Cure for Groups*. Through videos, discussion questions, and practical group applications, it guides you in creating a small group that's bursting with life, depth, and the kind of authentic community Jesus created us for.

TWO ROADS

Explore the first three chapters of *The Cure* in-depth with this small group study. *Two Roads* is designed to help your group travel beyond the mask and start experiencing real, authentic relationships through videos, discussion questions, scripture, and application.

Based on *The Cure*, Chapters 1-3.

CRAZY-MAKING

Have you ever kept doing something you don't want to do? We all have these patterns in our lives that we just can't seem to shake. In this four-week study, you'll explore where these patterns come from, why we keep repeating them, and how to stop the crazy and live in the freedom Jesus made possible.

Based on *The Cure*, Chapter 4.

HEALING RELATIONSHIPS

We all have experienced the pain of broken relationships, whether we hurt others or they hurt us. While many of us have been told to forgive or repent through gritted teeth and willpower, few of us have been shown how to offer forgiveness or repentance that overflows from our new hearts. Explore the path to freedom and healing Jesus provides in this four-part group study.

Based on *The Cure*, Chapter 5.

THE HEART OF MAN PARTICIPANT GUIDE

A companion study guide to unpack and process the film The Heart of Man (available online and at Trueface.org), this Trueface resource includes contributions from Jackie Hill Perry, Dan Allender, WM Paul Young, Jay Stringer, and John and Stasi Eldredge. Join us in experiencing the love of the Father in the midst of our darkest struggles.

BOOKS

THE CURE

Unpacking our view of ourselves and our view of God, *The Cure* invites you to remove your mask and experience God's lavish grace. This flagship book explores identity, community, sin, healing, destiny, and more as you discover that maybe God isn't who you think he is . . . and neither are you.

BOOKS

THE CURE FOR GROUPS

Do you want the kind of small group people will talk about the rest of their lives? A practical guide to starting (or re-igniting) your group, *The Cure for Groups* unpacks five Core Components to build a group that's bursting with life, depth, and the kind of life-changing community Jesus modeled for us.

THE CURE AND PARENTS

Travel with the Clawson family on their summer vacation as they struggle to navigate their family dynamics. Told partly through narrative and partly through teaching, this resource is for anyone wanting to bring grace to their family.

TRUST FOR TODAY

This 365-day devotional invites you to experience grace in your daily life, both in the big moments and the details of life. Use these short readings to incorporate grace into your everyday.

BO'S CAFÉ

Steven Kerner is living the dream in southern California, until his wife kicks him out after another angry outburst. Walk with Steven and his eccentric mentor Andy as they explore Steven's unresolved problems and performance-based life, rediscovering the restoration and healing only God's grace can provide.

THE ASCENT OF A LEADER

Become the leader people want to follow by opening yourself up to the influences that develop character: enduring relationships with friends, family, and God. *The Ascent of a Leader* guides you through cultivating extraordinary character in your home, company, community, and every other arena of life.

BEHIND THE MASK

When sin enters our lives, we have automatic, God-given responses. If we are the one who sinned, our response is guilt. If we are sinned against, our response is hurt. Explore these two involuntary responses and how they can lead to painful patterns of hiding and hurting, unless we allow the grace of Jesus to heal us.